ON YOUR BIKE

Contents

Why cycle? 2	Roundabouts and overtaking....18
Know your bike 4	Where to ride off-road 20
Types of bikes......................6	Off-road riding skills................22
Clothing 8	Maintenance and safety 24
Accessories 10	Theft, security and insurance ...26
Rules of the road................12	Further information................28
Setting off 14	Glossary 30
Turning left and right 16	Index 32

Written by Peter McGrath
Photographed by Chris Fairclough

Collins Educational
An Imprint of HarperCollinsPublishers

WHY CYCLE?

Nothing can beat a good bike ride. Hurtling down a hill or pedalling along a country lane with the wind behind you is a wonderful feeling; it is great fun, but there are plenty of other reasons why you should get on your bike:

● Cycling is good for you. It is one of the best forms of exercise because it burns up lots of energy, strengthens muscles (including the heart), and makes you feel good. Regular cyclists live longer and are usually fitter than non-cyclists.

● Cycling also benefits the environment, because it is a form of transport which does not cause pollution. Each car on the road pours tons of polluting gas into the air each year, and some doctors blame vehicle exhaust fumes for causing increased levels of asthma.

● Cycling is fast. Bikes can usually move at a brisk pace, whatever the weather or however congested the roads.

● Cycling is practical. Seventy-two percent of all journeys are less than five miles long, a distance that can be cycled in about half an hour. You can hang a pannier on your bike to hold your school books, swimming gear, sports equipment or shopping.

● Cycling is cheap. Once you have bought your bike it is very cheap to maintain it. Using a bike for everyday journeys will save on bus fares and you can be independent. No more waiting for parents to finish what they're doing before giving you a lift.

So, if cycling is fun, good for you, good for the environment, fast, practical and cheap, why not do it?

Before you start, however, you need to know how to make the most of your bike. You could just jump on it, and ride with the saddle at the wrong height, a rusty chain or without brakes. You could pedal the wrong way, leave it too long in the garden to go rusty or ride with a bag hanging over the handlebars just asking for a crash, but this book tells you how to avoid these mistakes.

Read on to find out how to choose the right bicycle, how to ride it properly and how to enjoy it for the rest of your life.

KNOW YOUR BIKE

There are many different kinds of bicycle, so what is shown here is a 'hybrid' which shares looks and equipment from both on- and off-road bikes. A bike is not a toy although it gives lots of enjoyment. If you want to get the best out of your bike, recognising the various parts will help you to ride it properly and keep it in good condition.

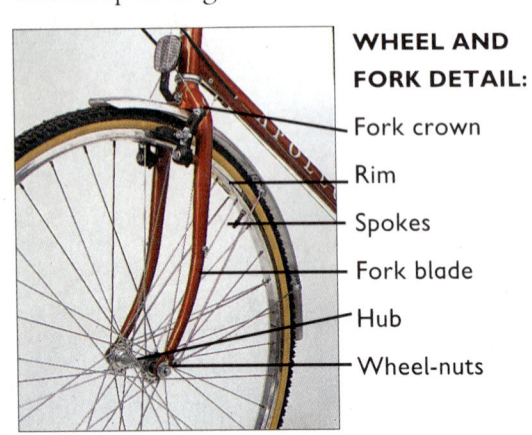

WHEEL AND FORK DETAIL:
- Fork crown
- Rim
- Spokes
- Fork blade
- Hub
- Wheel-nuts

BRAKE DETAIL:
- Brake cable
- Straddle wire
- Brake block
- Cantilever arm

5

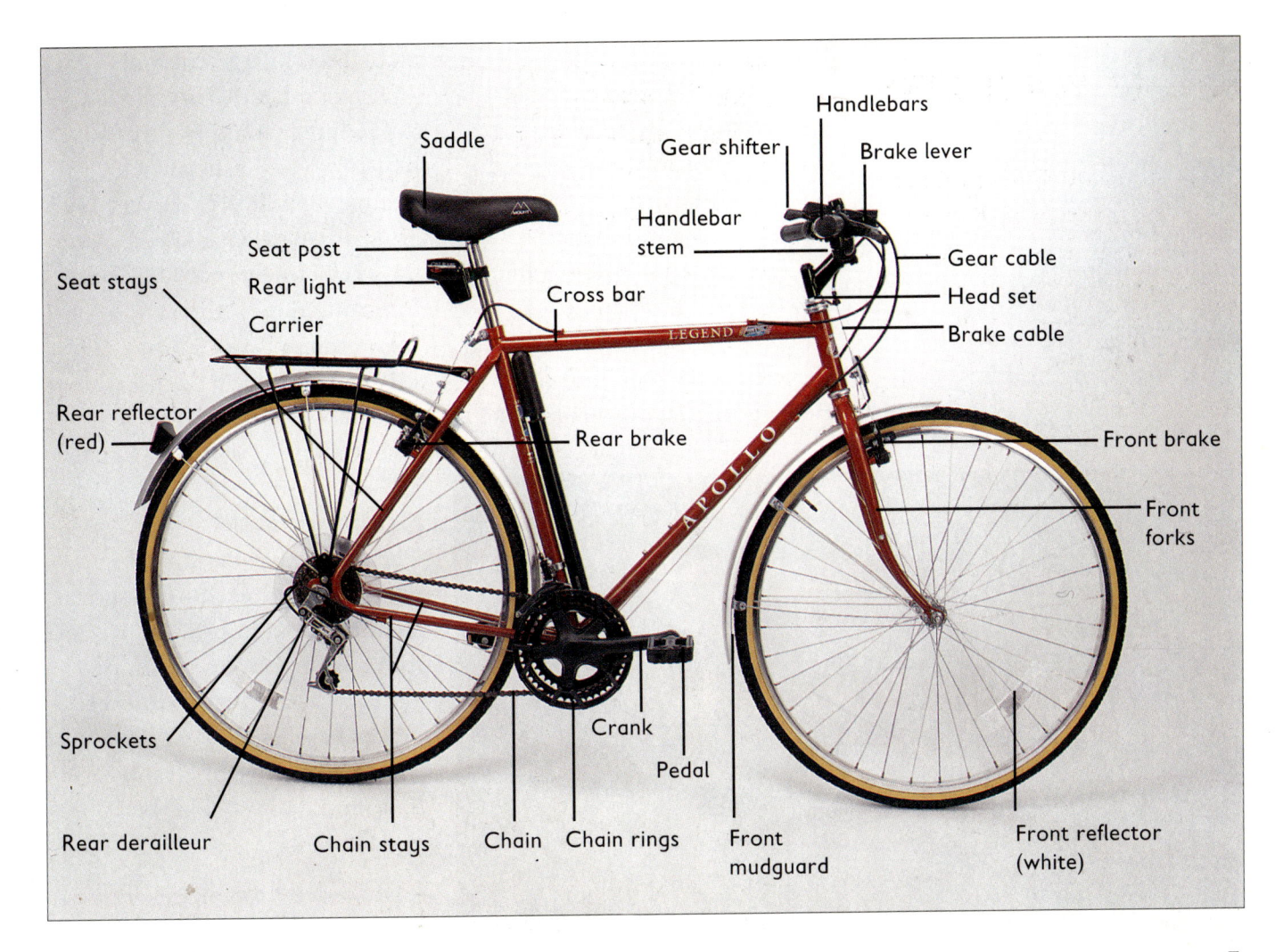

Types of bikes

Different types of bikes are made for different types of cycling. Two of the best known types of bikes are racing bikes and mountain bikes. Both are really racing bikes – one designed for road racing, the other for racing on forest trails and mountain tracks.

Racing bikes
These have thin, high pressure tyres to minimise rolling resistance for maximum speed on smooth tarmac.

Racing bikes don't have mudguards, which slow a bike down. They have compact, efficient calliper brakes. Racing bicycles need good brakes – a rider in the *Tour de France* can race down hills at 80kmh!

Dropped handlebars allow a streamlined riding position, reducing wind resistance.

Super-fit riders push very high gears at an amazing speed. They use very closely spaced gears to fine-tune their effort.

The frame is made from light, stiff materials such as special steel alloys, aluminium or carbon-fibre.

Mountain bikes
These have fat, knobbly, low pressure tyres that absorb shocks from bumps and provide grip on rough, loose surfaces and mud. Fat tyres mean that cantilever brakes have to be fitted. The frame has plenty of clearance so that mud doesn't clog the wheels.

A racing bike is built for speed with dropped handlebars, thin tyres and no mudguards

Straight handlebars give maximum control over obstacles that would usually knock the wheel sideways.

Big frame tubes make a tough frame that can survive crash damage.

Neither of these bikes are suitable for riding to school and genuine machines are also very expensive. What you see in the shops are bikes made to look like them and with some of the capabilities. These are sports bikes (drop-handlebar racing lookalikes) and all terrain bikes (ATBs) with flat handlebars and chunky tyres. The more like the real thing they are, the lighter the bike will be and the more expensive they become.

An ATB can be ridden on the road as well as on tracks and bridleways. Don't be fooled by a tough-looking cheap ATB – they can be heavy and awkward to ride. To get somewhere quickly, use a sports bike.

TOURERS AND HYBRIDS

Most people need something between the two extremes – a touring bike or a hybrid bike. A tourer looks like a racing bike, but is more robust, comfortable and can carry luggage. A hybrid looks like an ATB with flat handlebars but with lighter wheels. Both tourers and hybrids are excellent for riding on the road and can cope with tracks and trails too.

ROADSTERS

These are old-fashioned, slow, reliable, tough and very practical. Millions of people all over the world depend on this type of bike for everyday transport. The basic design hasn't changed much in 100 years, because a roadster is easy to make and cheap to maintain.

SMALL-WHEELERS

Bikes for smaller people need smaller wheels. Examples of small-wheelers are a BMX or a junior-sized ATB. These bikes are designed to be easy to maintain. Small wheels are also used on folding bikes.

Small-wheelers are easy to ride and easy to maintain

7

CLOTHING

Most bicycle trips are very short so it doesn't really matter what clothing is worn. However, on a ride that is more than two miles long, it is sensible to dress correctly. For racing, mountain-biking or longer rides proper cycling clothes should be worn.

For everyday riding, don't wear loose clothes – baggy trousers or a billowy skirt can become tangled in the chain or spokes of the rear wheel and make pedalling more difficult by increasing wind resistance.

KEEPING WARM:
Cycling is very energetic, and even on a chilly day you warm up quickly. Dress in several thin layers rather than one thick pullover.

KEEPING DRY:
A waterproof jacket is usually enough for everyday use. Roll it up and keep it in the pannier or saddlebag.

THE EVERYDAY CYCLIST TOP-TO-TOE:
Helmet:
Helmets are designed to protect the head from injury in low-speed crashes which can occur in bad weather if the roads are slippery. However, a helmet will not keep you completely safe; you must also ride safely and be alert at all times.

Top-half:
T-shirt, sweatshirt and gloves. If you get hot, whip off the sweatshirt; if you are chilly put another layer on. Wear gloves if it is cold. There is nothing more miserable than freezing hands.

Cycling gloves have tough, padded palms to protect the hands in a fall.

Reflective strips and patches:
These come in fluorescent colours to increase visibility during the day and are reflective to show up in car headlights at night. You need to be noticed by other road users at all times.

Bottom half:
Jeans are uncomfortable for cycling. Leggings and tracksuit bottoms are ideal as they move with the body instead of rubbing against the skin.

Shoes:
Stiff-soled shoes are best. Floppy-soled shoes will bend as the pedal is pushed down, wasting energy.

RIGHT AND WRONG CLOTHING

✓

✗

Always wear a helmet. Tie back long hair.

Sweatshirts and T-shirts are ideal – they move with the body.

Reflective strips and patches help other road users see you.

Dress in layers – if you get too hot you can peel one off.

Leggings move with the body and cannot get trapped in the chain.

Stiff-soled shoes help you pedal more efficiently.

Never wear a floppy hat – the brim could fall over your eyes.

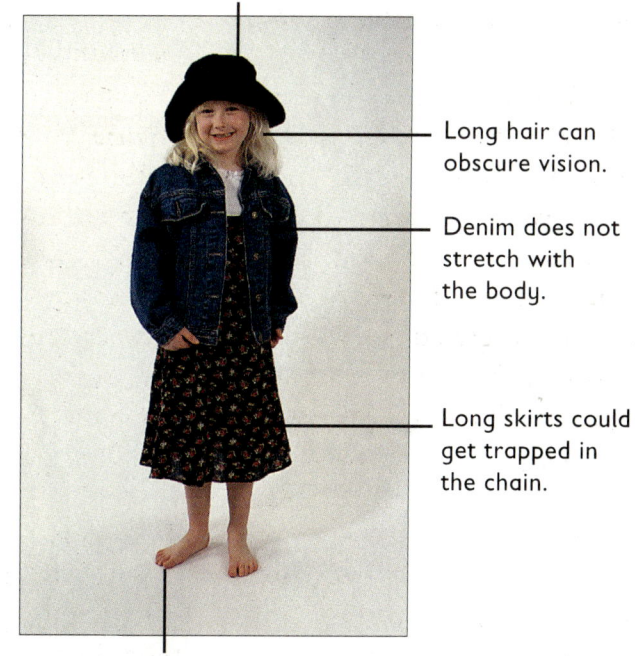

Long hair can obscure vision.

Denim does not stretch with the body.

Long skirts could get trapped in the chain.

Never cycle barefoot – you could lose your toes!

9

ACCESSORIES

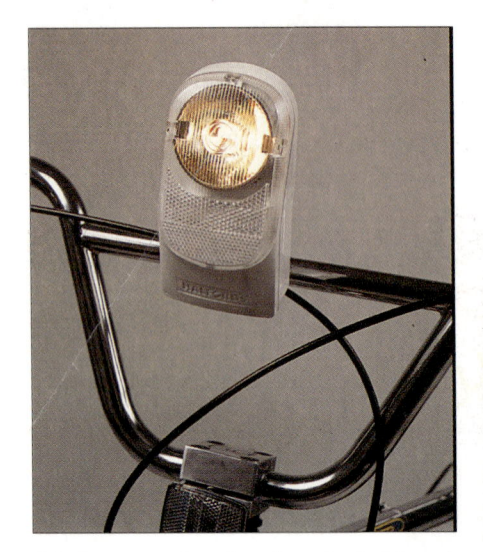

Lights are absolutely vital. Use them at night and on gloomy days so that other road users can see you.

Battery lights show a good beam at first but become dimmer as the battery is used up. They can be expensive to run and are easily stolen if left on your bike.

Dynamo lights work by electricity generated during pedalling. While you are moving they produce a good beam of light, but at junctions they cut out, so many cyclists use a red flashing Light Emitting Diode (LED) pointing backwards to warn car drivers and cyclists driving up behind.

Carrying rack and panniers: These transform a bicycle into a useful, practical form of

Panniers can be used to carry school books, sports kit or shopping

transport as they carry loads — shopping, school books, sports kit — easily and safely. A rucksack could be used for small loads, but they can be uncomfortable. Never ride with a bag slung over the handlebars.

Bell:
A bike moves quickly and is very quiet so it is easy for a pedestrian to step in the way without seeing it. A friendly ring from a bell lets everyone know that a cyclist is coming.

A Sam Browne belt:
This slings across one shoulder and fastens around the waist. Most are brightly coloured for daytime use and reflective at night. Reflective arm and leg-bands are also available, as are a number of brightly coloured fluorescent patches.

Mudguards:
Wet roads are covered in filth and without mudguards clothes will be ruined and chains and gears clogged up. Also, anyone riding behind you will be showered in muck from the rear wheel. Unless you have a real racing bike, fit mudguards.

Water bottle and cage:
Cycling can be very thirsty

Always carry a full water bottle on long, energetic rides

work. For longer rides, a cage bolted to the frame and a water bottle means that you can drink on the move.

Prop-stand:
There is usually something to lean a bike against, so a stand is not vital — it is just more weight to pedal around.

11

Rules of the Road

Most cycling is done on the roads amongst cars, lorries and buses. By knowing the rules of the road and learning how to ride a bike in traffic, you will be able to ride safely and enjoyably. The best way to learn is to watch an experienced cyclist ride on the road. Start on quiet roads and don't progress to busy roads without feeling completely confident or without an adult's permission.

Golden rules:
- Concentrate all the time – don't let your attention slip for a second.
- Make sure that your bicycle is in good condition, especially the brakes.

Worn brake blocks could be very dangerous – change them as soon as you notice any wear

- Dress sensibly. Choose clothing that is comfortable and won't catch in the chain or wheel. Wear something bright to help other road users to see you.
- If you ride at night, make sure that you have working lights and a set of reflectors.
- Do not ride in the gutter – the safest place is about one metre away from the kerb. This way you will avoid rubbish and broken glass and car drivers will be able to see you.
- Always signal before turning left, right or slowing down. Don't just flash out your hand – stick out your whole arm in a long, clear signal well before you turn.
- Watch everyone else's signals so you know what they are going to do.
- Read the Highway Code to learn what traffic signs and road markings mean.
- If your school runs a cycle training course, do it.

Fit your bike with a set of lights

Setting off

Wherever you ride, there are problems to overcome, but keeping alert will help you to spot the problems long before reaching them.

Before you go:
Don't just jump on the bike and set off. Take a few seconds to check that the tyres are hard, the brakes work perfectly and the wheels are securely attached to the rest of the bike.

Setting off:
With the bike stationary on the road, check behind to see if there is a gap in the traffic. Whilst doing this, have your arm out giving a clear 'Right Turn' signal. When a gap in the traffic occurs, pedal off and ride one metre away from the kerb.

Riding straight ahead:
Be bold! Ride one metre from the kerb at all times. It is the best place to be seen by car drivers. Always ride in a confident, straight line.

Glance over your shoulder regularly. You need to know what is happening on the road behind. Keep an eye open for cars indicating that they are about to turn left. They might overtake you, then suddenly cut across your path. Always keep your fingers close to the brake levers, ready to slow down or stop.

Keep an eye on the road look out for:
● **Oil** – where oil spills on a

Always check the tyres and brakes before you set off

wet road, it looks like a shiny, rainbow-coloured splash. It could be slippery. Avoid it.

● **Gravel** – will cause a skid.

● **Potholes** – can shake you,

jolt you off and could easily damage your bike.

● **Broken glass** – can produce a sudden flat tyre.

● **Pedestrians** – can sometimes step off the pavement right in front of you. Use a bell to warn them you are coming and be ready to brake.

● **Parked cars** – when overtaking a parked car, watch out in case the door opens suddenly or a hidden pedestrian steps out in to the road from behind it.

POTHOLES:
Before long you are bound to see a pothole. If possible, squeeze to the left of the hole, but if there is not enough room, don't panic and swerve into the traffic. Check over your shoulder and, if the road is clear, signal right and pedal around the pothole as though overtaking a parked car. If there is not room to pedal around the pothole, brake gently, raise your bottom off the saddle and go through the pothole, letting the bike take the shock of the bump.

Try to avoid potholes as they can damage your bike

15

Turning left and right

You have to be able to turn left and right with confidence. Learn how to do this with an experienced rider on a quiet road. The golden road rules apply:

Be alert.
- Be observant – check behind you regularly.

- Signal clearly, well ahead of the turn.

Turning left:
Turning left is easy because you don't have to cross a stream of traffic. Signal clearly, thirty metres before the turn. Glance over your shoulder to make sure that no-one is following too closely. Maintain the signal until just before starting to turn, then put both hands firmly on the handlebars as you steer through the turn.

Turning left into a main road

Look out for:
Loose gravel. Gravel often collects on bends, and if you see some, try to avoid it. If you do ride over gravel DON'T grab the brakes – you'll definitely fall off.

TURNING RIGHT:
Turning right in traffic is a difficult but very important manoeuvre to learn to do properly and with confidence. It requires a move across traffic that might be about to overtake you. Well ahead of the right turn, check behind. Wait for a gap in the traffic, signal right and move across the carriageway into the middle of the road. Ride until you reach the turn-off. If the road is clear, turn right.

If there is traffic coming, stop. The bike should be in a low gear, read to power you away. Have your right arm out, signalling to oncoming traffic that you want to turn right. Wait for a clear gap in the traffic, and pedal into the right turn quickly, smoothly and under control.

Turning right into a main road

Sometimes, a car will wait and flash its lights at you – this means that they are inviting you to cross in front of them, but before you do, make sure other drivers are aware of what is happening. If a right-hand turn looks really busy, signal left, stop and push the bike across the road using the Green Cross Code.

LOOK OUT FOR:
Cars coming up behind you.

17

Roundabouts and Overtaking

Roundabouts

Negotiating a roundabout needs confidence, good observation and control. There are many types of roundabout, so bear these general rules in mind and look at the diagrams on signalling on pages 16-17 and page 19.

If you are passing an exit, signal right to tell car drivers you are continuing on the roundabout. If you are using an exit (leaving the roundabout) signal left.

WARNING! Most car drivers are very bad at signalling on roundabouts, so it pays to be super alert.

Overtaking a parked car:

When riding on the road, you will need to move out to pass parked cars. Move out well before reaching the car, check over your shoulder to see if it is safe to move to the right.

Look for a gap in the traffic and put your right arm out in a clear signal. On passing the car, leave a one-metre gap between you and it. Watch the car just in case the driver opens the door in your path.

When cycling along a line of parked cars, don't weave in and out of the cars – keep riding in a straight line with the bike under close control.

Look out for:
- Parked cars with suddenly opening doors.
- Parked cars pulling out whilst you are riding past them.
- Pedestrians and dogs walking out from between parked cars.

Riding in traffic – do's and don'ts
- **Do** ride confidently.
- **Do** signal clearly before moving right or left.
- **Do** stay alert and be ready to brake or accelerate suddenly.
- **Do** look over your shoulder regularly.
- **Don't** wobble or weave about on your bike.
- **Don't** ride in the gutter.
- **Don't** take risks.
- **Don't** daydream.
- **Don't** ride with a bag slung over the handlebars.
- **Don't** ride on pavements. Pavements are for pedestrians, so if you have to cross a pavement, get off and push.
- **Don't** ride up the inside of a queue of traffic.

TURNING LEFT	**GOING STRAIGHT ON**	**TURNING RIGHT**
While approaching the roundabout, keep in the left-hand lane. Join the roundabout when there is a safe gap in the traffic, and stay in the left-hand lane. Signal left before your exit, and then as you turn keep both hands on the handlebars.	Whilst approaching the roundabout, keep in the left-hand lane. Join the roundabout when there is a safe gap in the traffic, staying in the left-hand lane as you go round. Watch out for traffic coming up behind you, or turning left in front of you. Signal before your exit, then make the turn keeping both hands on the handlebars.	To turn right on a roundabout, look, signal right, and position yourself in the right-hand side of your lane as you would for a right turn into a main road (see p.17). When there is a safe gap in the traffic, move out into the right-hand lane of the roundabout. Signal left before your exit, and then as you turn keep both hands on the handlebars.

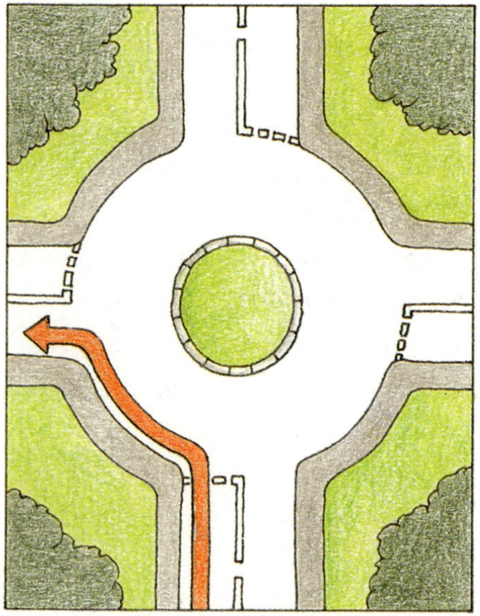

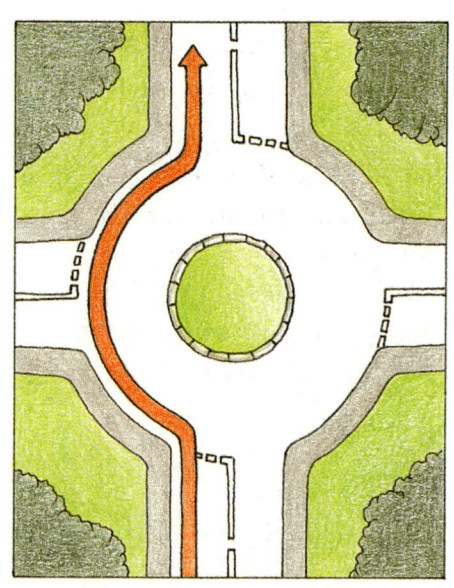

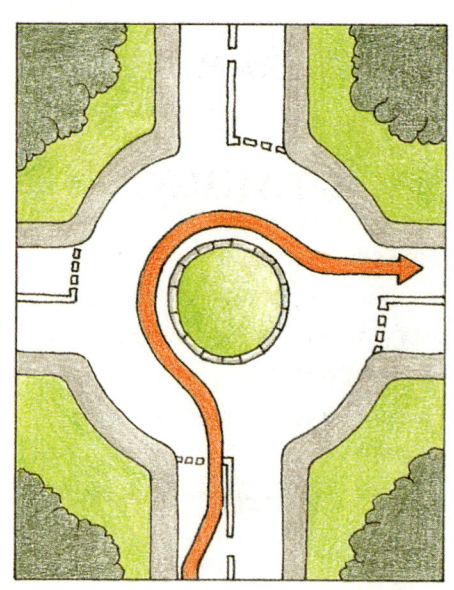

Where to ride off-road

All terrain bikes (ATBs) are designed to cope with muddy conditions, rough tracks, steep climbs and bumpy descents, but owning the right type of bike doesn't mean you can ride it wherever you like in the countryside. First you need to learn where you can ride off-road, and exactly how to do it.

Public land
You have a right of way – that is, you are allowed to ride – on bridleways and roads. On bridleways, give way to walkers and people on horses.

Canal towpaths
Many canal towpaths are open to cyclists – notices at the entrances tell you whether or not you can ride on them.

Cycle paths
You might live near a Sustrans cycle path. These are paths specially built for cyclists to use, where you can ride without worrying about cars. Your council might publish a leaflet telling you where any local bike paths are. Check in the library.

Public footpaths
These are for walkers and they are strictly out of bounds to cyclists. It may be tempting but never cycle on them.

A Sustrans cycle path in Bristol

Private land

If the landowner gives you permission, you can ride anywhere, but do remember that public footpaths cross private land and you can't use them for cycling.

The best way to plan a good off-road ride is to use a detailed Ordnance Survey map.

Off-road common sense

You are far more likely to fall off while riding off-road, so wear a helmet.
- Make sure the bike is in good condition – rattling along a forest trail is hard on the bike, so check that everything is properly tightened up and the brakes are in working order.
- Go with a friend and make sure that adults know where you are going and when to expect you back.
- Off-road cycling is very energetic, so take food and drink.
- Wear old clothes that can stand up to getting coated in mud and take a waterproof.
- In summer, protect yourself against sunburn.
- On canal towpaths, be careful to avoid boat mooring ropes and anglers' fishing gear that might be across the towpath.

Riding responsibly

Mountain biking is a lot of fun, but there are rules to obey in order to protect the countryside.
- Whenever you ride, follow the off-road code.
- Obey the law, do not cycle on public footpaths.
- Always close gates after going through them.
- Do not ride too fast – you never know who or what is around the next corner.
- Take your litter home. Leave the countryside as you find it.
- Do not light fires.
- Do not skid on tracks or they will quickly become eroded.
- Give way to horseriders and pedestrians.

Riding off-road is a wonderful experience. Although there are no cars or lorries, you share these tracks with other people who also want to enjoy them, so be considerate and polite when you meet pedestrians, horseriders and other cyclists.

OFF-ROAD RIDING SKILLS

Cycling off-road needs a different set of skills from road-riding. Cornering, braking, climbing and descending hills are all completely different when there is mud, gravel, tree roots, nettles, tractor ruts, overhanging branches and the odd stray cow to cope with.

GENERAL RIDING TIPS

Be prepared to spend a lot of time with your bottom off the saddle. Riding like this is called 'honking'.
- Keep a good grip on the handlebars.
- Use toeclips – you'll be more secure on the bike.
- Don't be tense – relax, and you will control the bike far more easily.
- Don't slam on the front brake when riding on loose surfaces.
- Use the gears. They are there to make pedalling easy, so select a gear where your legs are spinning, with enough in reserve to accelerate.
- Keep your head up and look well ahead, checking for obstacles.

BASIC OFF-ROAD TECHNIQUES

There are many books about how to ride a bike off-road, but the best way to learn is to go with an experienced off-road cyclist.

Downhill

Keep your bottom slightly off the saddle, a firm grip on the handlebars, arms slightly bent, feet in the toeclips and legs slightly bent. Have a couple of fingers on the brake levers, ready to brake and slow down, with the thumbs ready to change gear. You need a good grip on the handlebars – hitting a bump at speed will snatch the wheel and may jerk them out of your hand.

Learn to ride off-road with an experienced cyclist

Climbing

Keep your bottom on the saddle as much as possible – weight on the saddle means the back wheel will grip far better. Approaching the hill, change down through the gears so that the pedals spin freely at the foot of the hill. Beware of tackling a steep hill in a gear that is too low – the front wheel might lift off the ground.

When riding a bike off-road you are sure to encounter some difficulties. Don't be afraid to get off the bike, sling it over your shoulder and walk up a steep slope or around a difficult obstacle.

Cornering

Watch experienced mountain bikers going around corners. Beware of riding in ruts such as tractor tracks running along the bend. Be careful not to corner too fast – you could ride off the bend or let the bike slip from underneath you.

For sudden, sharp turns always rise off the saddle and turn the bike underneath you. The bike will 'fall' into the turn in a controlled manner, and your body will catch up as it goes into the turn.

Careful cornering in the wet

Braking

Braking while off-road riding needs a lot of practice. You need to control your speed, rather than jamming on brakes at the last minute.

Front brakes must be treated with care. Slamming on the front brake can lock the front wheel, which will slip the bike from under you.

If the track is firm, use the front brake as usual. On loose or wet surfaces, pump the brakes on and off so that the front wheel slows without locking.

Back brakes also need some care. If you are riding full pelt down a hill and grab at the back brake a rear-wheel skid will result. When using the back brake, make sure that you are sitting on the saddle or leaning off the back of it with your weight over the back wheel.

Maintenance and safety

Make sure the tyres are kept well pumped up

Your life can depend on the state of your bicycle, so keep it in good condition. With regular maintenance a bike is cheap to run. If you neglect it, leave it outside and fail to keep it up to scratch, it will rust and be difficult to ride. A well-maintained bike is a safe bike.

Some small maintenance jobs you can do yourself, but for major repair work use the local bike shop, where it will be repaired by an expert. Unless one of the family is a genius with bikes, take it into a bike shop for a service once a year.

Tyres
Tyres should be in good condition and well pumped up. Tyres with bald patches of tread or splits in the wall should be changed immediately.

Brakes
The brake-blocks should hit the rim squarely and should not squeal when the brake is applied. The brakes should be adjusted so that the wheel runs freely between the blocks when the brakes are off. Worn brake-blocks should be changed.

Cables
Brake and gear cables should

Use an old toothbrush to clean the chain and gears

Keep the chain clean and oiled

run smoothly. If a cable is sticking, it is because the cable is frayed or needs lubricating. A squirt of spray-lubricant or a few drops of oil allowed to run into the cable's outer cover will free a dried cable. A frayed cable should be replaced.

WHEELS
Wheels should spin freely and the nuts that hold them into the frame should be tight.

CHAIN
Never let the chain get rusty. Use an old toothbrush to clean the chain and gears. Give the chain a good squirt of lubricant and use the toothbrush to scrub off grit and oil. Give the chain another good spray, wait for the lubricant to drip off, then apply a dribble of oil or special cycle-chain lubricant.

GEARS
Derailleur gears take a lot of punishment. They should be scrubbed and oiled when you lubricate your chain. When you are riding, the gears should run quietly. If there is a grating noise check that the cage of the front derailleur is not rubbing against the chain.

A rattle from the back could mean that the indexing is out of adjustment, or that the chain and sprockets are worn. Worn chain and sprockets usually make the chain jump when pressure is put on the pedals. Attending to this is not usually something that can be done at home – it is a job for the local bike shop.

Theft, security and insurance

There are 500,000 bicycles stolen every year, so to keep yours safe, precautions should be taken. Never leave the bicycle unlocked. Whenever you go out on the bike, take a lock with you and whenever the bike is out of your sight, lock it up.

Cycle security
- Lock it in a well-lit public place.
- Lock it to something solid – a set of railings, a lamp post or a bicycle parking rack.
- Take the pump and lights away with you.
- If the front wheel is quick-release, lock it to the rest of the bike or take it with you.

Types of lock
D lock or shackle lock
A hard metal D locks into a cross-piece with a special thief-resistant lock. These are the best locks that you can buy, but they are expensive and heavy to carry. For this reason, D locks have brackets so that the lock can be attached to the frame.

Cable lock
A cable lock is a long, thick piece of steel wire. The two ends lock together, allowing both the wheels and frame to be fixed to a solid object, but it is less secure than a D lock.

Padlock and chain
These can either be very flimsy

Always take a cycle lock with you and use it whenever you leave your bike

26

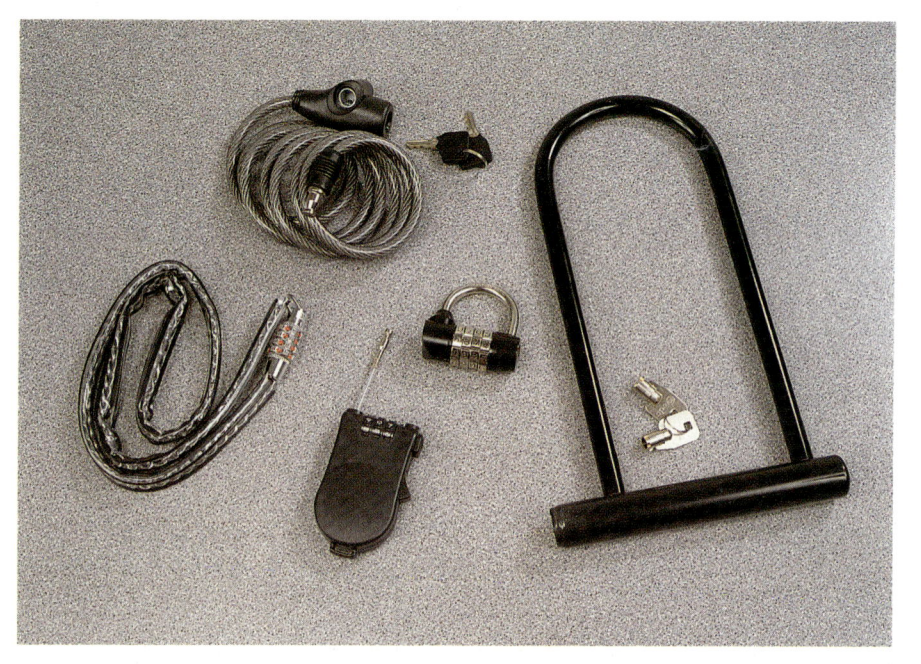

HOW TO LOCK THE BIKE
Find a lamp post or railings, lean the bike close to it and pass the lock through the frame, around the post, through the back wheel and lock it. If the chain or the cable lock is long enough, lock the front wheel as well. If the front wheel is quick-release, undo it and lean it next to the frame so that it can be locked to the rest of the bike. If the saddle has a quick-release clamp, take it with you.

INSURANCE
Bicycles can be added to the household contents insurance, or there are special bicycle insurance schemes available to members of the Cyclists' Touring Club, see page 28.

or massive heavy chains with strong locks. The stronger they are, the heavier they are to carry. Some are made especially for bicycle security and the chain is covered in a plastic sleeve to protect the bike paintwork.

Combination locks
A combination lock has a secret number that must be dialled into the lock to open it (see above, centre). Most combination locks are flimsy and are best avoided.

27

Further Information

Books

One of the best books about bikes and cycling is *Richards New Bicycle Book*, by Richard Ballantine and Richard Grant. This is the all-in-one book about buying, riding, repairing and owning a bike.

For anyone wishing to attempt some DIY, *Richards Bicycle Repair Manual* is an excellent introduction manual.

Clubs

Whether you just go for short rides at the weekends, ride your mountain bike off-road or want to race on-road, there are cyclists' clubs to help. Your local bike shop will be able to tell you where the nearest bike clubs are. Some clubs have junior or family sections so that you can take part in rides or races with people of your own age.

The British Cyclists' Federation is in charge of road-racing in Britain. Contact the BCF for information on the nearest road-racing club.

The Cyclists' Touring Club is the club for everyday cyclists, including mountain bikers. Being a member of the CTC means that you are insured whenever you ride your bike. Your bike is insured, you can join their local clubs free and will receive the club magazine six times a year. The CTC also runs National Bike Week, which promotes cycling to the public through a week-long series of events in June. Schools are welcome to become involved, and the free National Bike Week Event Organisers' Guide describes events that can be held by schools to encourage safe cycling among pupils.

Useful Addresses

British Cyclists' Federation
National Cycling Centre
Stuart Street
Manchester
M11 4DQ

Cyclists' Touring Club
69 Meadrow
Godalming
Surrey
GU7 3HS
Tel: 01483 417217

To get involved in National Bike Week write to:

National Bike Week
69 Meadrow
Godalming
Surrey
GU7 3HS
Tel: 01483 414346

For more information about cycling write to:

The Bicycle Association
Starley House
Eaton Road
Coventry
CV1 2FH

The Bicycle Association publishes a range of leaflets about cycling which can be sent for.

Glossary

ATB: All Terrain Bike. A bicycle built to be ridden off-road. Also known as a mountain bike, an all terrain bike has fat, knobbly tyres, powerful brakes, a tough frame and a wide range of gears.

Bridleway: A public right of way. Bridleways can be used by walkers, horseriders and pedestrians, and are marked on maps.

Chain rings: The large-toothed rings at the front of the chain. There may be one, two or three on your bike.

Cranks: The cranks attach the pedals to the chain rings.

Derailleur: When you change gear, the derailleur moves the chain from one sprocket or chain ring to the next. Derailleurs are also called changers or mechs.

Fluorescent: Fluorescent clothes have been dyed with special chemicals that make them glow.

Highway Code: A book that tells drivers, cyclists, motorcyclists, horseriders and pedestrians how to behave on the road.

Hybrid bicycle: A bicycle that looks like an ATB, but shares some of the features of a road bike.

LED: Light Emitting Diode. A flashing or steady red light that can be used as a back-up for the dynamo or battery-powered back light.

Mountain bike: Another name for an All Terrain Bike.

Pannier: A bag that has been specially designed to fit on a bicycle to carry luggage. Panniers hook onto a carrying rack that is fitted over the bike's rear wheel.

Pedestrians: Walkers.

Public footpath: A right of way that is not a road, which can only be used by pedestrians.

Reflectors: Reflectors shine light back from where it came. In a car's headlights, light will be reflected back from any reflectors attached to the bike or on clothing.

Rolling resistance: A bike's tyres stick to the road as they roll along. Narrow high-pressure tyres stick less and roll faster, while fat ATB tyres stick to the road more.

Sustrans: Short for 'sustainable transport'. This organisation is setting up a network of cycleways across the UK.

Touring bicycle: A bicycle with drop handlebars specially made for long rides and taking on holiday as it can carry plenty of luggage.

Wind resistance: When pedalling most of the effort goes into pushing air aside. Air is difficult to push aside, and 80 percent of pedalling energy goes into beating wind resistance.

INDEX

Accessories 10
ATBs 7,20

Bell 11,15
Bicycle Association, The 29
Brakes, braking .2,4,5,6,12,14,15
,16,18,19,20,22,23,24
BMX 7
British Cyclists' Federation 27,28

Cable lock 26,27
Cables 24
Canal towpaths 20,21
Carrying rack 10
Chain . .2,5,8,9,11,13,25,26,27
Climbing 22,23
Clothing 8,9,13,30
Combination locks 27
Cornering 22,23
Cycle paths 20
Cycling books 28
Cyclists' Touring Club . . .27,28

Derailleur gears 5,25
D lock 26
Downhill 22
Dropped handlebars 6
Gears 6,11,22,23,25

Golden Rules 12
Green Cross Code 17

Handlebars2,5,6,7,11,16,18,19,22
Helmets 8,9,21
Highway Code 13
Hybrid bike 4,7

Insurance 26,27

Lights 5,10,13,26
Locks 26
Lubricant 25

Maintenance 24
Mountain bikes 6,28,30
Mudguards 5,6,11

National Bike Week 28,29

Off-road 4,20,21,22,23,28
Oil 14,25
Overtaking 15,18

Padlock 26
Panniers 2,8,10
Parked cars 15,18
Pedestrians 11,15,18,21
Potholes 14,15
Private land 21

Prop-stand 11
Public land 20

Racing bikes 6,7,11
Reflective strips 8,9
Roadsters 7
Roundabouts 18,19
Rules of the road 12

Safety 24
Sam Browne belt 11
Security 26,27
Setting off 14
Shackelock – see D lock
Shoes 8,9
Signalling .13,14,15,16,17,18,19
Small-wheelers 7
Sports bikes 7
Sustrans 20

Theft 26
Tourers 7
Turning left 13,16,19
Turning right 17,19
Tyres 6,7,14,15,24

Waterproof jacket 8,21
Wheels 4,6,7,8,11,13,14,22,
23,24,25,26,27